haiku-vision

I am one / who eats his breakfast / gazing at the morning-glories. / Bashô

haiku-vision

in poetry and photography

Ann Atwood

Charles Scribner's Sons New York

To you, Marcia

With deep appreciation to Baido Wakita
for the haiku translations and calligraphy
in the haigas on pages 14 and 15.

Library of Congress Cataloging in Publication Data

Atwood, Ann.
Haiku-vision.

SUMMARY: A collection of the author's haiku accompanies text and color photographs which explore the application of Japanese art and poetry to photography.
1. Haiku—Technique. 2. Haiku in photography. 3. Haiku, American. 4. Haiga. 5. Aesthetics, Japanese.
[1. Haiku. 2. Haiku in photography. 3. Haiga.]
I. Title.
PL729.A89 895.6'1'5 76-42287
ISBN 0-684-14858-7

1 3 5 7 9 11 13 15 17 19 YD/C 20 18 16 14 12 10 8 6 4 2

Printed in the United States of America

I am one
who eats his breakfast
gazing at the morning-glories.

Bashô

In this haiku Bashô expresses the state of total absorption necessary in all forms of creative activity, to which poetry and photography belong.

Out of Bashô's gazing came some of the greatest haiku in Japanese literature. These brief poems, written in the seventeenth century, were laced with "hidden glimmerings," bright glimpses into the secret network of nature where all things are interrelated. Bashô gazed at the morning-glory with such an intensity of vision that he felt the flower opening within himself.

Haiku is the fusion of seeing and feeling. What makes haiku unique among art forms is that all elaboration of ideas and descriptions has been eliminated so that this seeing-feeling can be instantly and spontaneously experienced. The spontaneity native to photography makes the camera an effective instrument in developing haiku-vision. But haiku must be felt as well as seen, and only by attempting to discover how such an emotional response can be evoked will we be able to pursue the elusive haiku in photography as well as poetry.

Haiku is the flower of an Eastern culture which for centuries has practiced the unhurried art of gazing. To understand how foreign such a culture is to our own, we have only to imagine ourselves meeting with friends to spend long hours of the night simply "moon-viewing," feeling the moon's presence, reflecting...remembering...imagining...

If we spoke at all, it might be of the frailness of petals, or of all the fleeting beauty in the world which so often goes unseen. A haiku is that one particular moon or flower which is quietly "gazed upon" until by recognition and reflection it is transformed into poetry.

A weightless balloon
slips from the hand of a child–
the wandering moon.

Two things the moon steals:
a light from the trunks of the trees,
a day from my life.

The first drop of rain
on the just-opened blossoms—
how the branch trembles!

The brook moves slowly
carrying the petalled cargo
of another spring.

In Japanese haiku there are many words which symbolize the seasons—and these words give the reader an immediate sense of time and mood.

The word for "plum blossoms" not only personifies spring, but also suggests the tenderness of love. When the word *deer* appears, it is swiftly fleeing autumn with its overtones of imminent change. The word *snow* indicates winter, but also means "the going," and here again the word defines both an image and an emotion.

Even without these season words and the feelings which they arouse we all respond to the changes in nature, for we ARE nature, and experience within ourselves the daily and yearly cycles of the earth.

Scenes of winter and spring, of sunrise and sunset affect us in themselves, but when we introduce a symbol such as deer into an autumn landscape, or homing birds into a scene at dusk, we strengthen both the mood and the image of our words and pictures.

Birds circling at dusk.
The first night of my journey–
yet how far from home!

Over the leaf-crisp ground
the deer in the autumn wood
leap...and make no sound.

Autumn already....
Summer's deer are bursts of brown
hiding in swiftness.

Now turning homeward
the fisherman feeling his catch
light on his shoulders.

Early haiga, or haiku-drawings, attempted to do in line and mass what haiku poetry attempted in image and implication. Haiga appeared at the beginning of the seventeenth century when Zen monks, using a calligraphic, or handwriting, style of painting, included the words of the haiku as an integral part of the picture.

Haiga, like haiku, were brief and highly suggestive, for haiku presented an image which evoked an emotion without describing the emotion itself. Each recognized space as a positive element, emphasizing that what was not said was as essential as what was said.

In a few spontaneous strokes and words, haiga sought to express not form alone, but the true spirit of the subject.

Shadows and silhouettes are in themselves a kind of haiga, for by eliminating detail they transform the personal into the universal. Their dark, broad strokes often convey some particular mood or inner quality of the subject, which is the aim of haiga.

Through darkening trees
the heron hunched on the rail
is already night.

Bashô created many haiga, yet neither his art nor his poetry affected the character of the Japanese haiku as much as his manner of living, which became the model of the haiku-life.

Freeing himself of all ties and possessions, Bashô made many long and lonely journeys, determined to take nothing from life but its meaning.

He lived in and with nature, finding eternity in every moment, and aware that his affinity with the most ordinary leaf, or the smallest of creatures, was one of deep significance.

Darting their lives away
the bright fish circling the pond
leave only patterns.

The day dark with rain.
Young leaves struggling to open,
you too have your tears.

Bashô discovered in every event in nature a correspondence within himself. To him landscapes had become inscapes which revealed the pure spirit of the tree or flower.

Bashô understood that state of illumination described by one of the Zen masters as "insight into the very nature of things, which now appear as so many fairy-like flowers having no graspable realities."

The camera, quite unexpectedly, gives us glimpses of such inscapes. Often through close-up or soft-focus lenses we can sense the essence of a simple weed or a common geranium.

"...as so many fairy-like flowers..."

The camera moves quite naturally into another realm of haiku—that of time and motion. For in shutter-like fashion, haiku slows down time or stops it altogether by crystallizing the immediate moment.

Yet once again there is that further step to be taken by the reader, the writer, the photographer—the effort, not merely to manipulate the moment, but to lift it out of time into timelessness.

Day flows into sea.
A girl and a boy on a rock
watching in silence.

A meadow-sculpture:
"Girl on an ivory stallion"
carved by the camera.

Haiku is an intuitive art which, through the use of many abstract elements, boldly and offhandedly attempts to convey the inexpressible.

In all oriental art the unexpressed and the inexpressible play an important part in aesthetic feeling, for they create in us an unconscious tension which quickens our perception.

This tension can be caused by as simple a thing as a split in the clouds when a dark landscape is subjected to the extreme contrast of momentary light.

A sense of the inexpressible is also present at those junctures in nature where the transient intercepts the eternal, and where the small is superimposed upon the great.

The image of a bird soaring alone in an infinite sky, or a sailboat adrift on the vastness of the sea, produces a certain poetic pressure in which seeing and feeling become one.

For an instant the gull
seemed to have charted its flight
on the rainbow's path.

The boats on the sea
halved by the swell of the waves
are now only sails.

The feeling of transience, of the fleetingness of things, is one of the underlying moods of Japanese art. It is felt in the melancholy browns of oriental paintings, and is symbolized in haiku by the word *dew.* It is also inherent in the image of *foam* which fades as quickly as it appears.

There are several moods in Zen which have become part of the atmosphere of haiku, particularly *wabi, sabi, aware,* and *yugen.* These are moods of loneliness, of aloneness, of longing, but not necessarily of sadness.

In *aware* there is a haunting sense of the past—not a nostalgia for that which has vanished, but a feeling that things, having once existed, cast an afterglow over the present.

The bells in the village
as the sun strikes the ruins
of an ancient church!

In *yugen* there is the recognition that nature is both mysterious and remote, a feeling that one is seeing the world through rays of mist. It is an awareness of the never-to-be-known, which brings with it a longing for the unattainable. *Yugen* is the sensation of the purity of light, when light is used in direct contrast to darkness.

In haiku poetry, *yugen* implies thoughts and emotions which are not easily understood. They appear in the poem only as vague impressions open to many interpretations.

In haiku-photography, familiar scenes which are photographed through clouds and mist suddenly become unfamiliar and take on this quality of *yugen* with its aura of mystery.

The boy in the foam....
Seeing him I touch the mist
veiling my childhood.

The fog fills the air.
The woods I knew are other woods–
is my neighbor there?

Yugen is the sensation of the purity of light.

The swan drifts away
gathering in its feathers
the light of the day.